She Persisted

DEB HAALAND

—INSPIRED BY—

She Persisted

by Chelsea Clinton & Alexandra Boiger

. . . .

DEB HAALAND

. . . .

Written by
Laurel Goodluck

Interior illustrations by
Gillian Flint

PHILOMEL

PHILOMEL
An imprint of Penguin Random House LLC, New York

First published in the United States of America by Philomel,
an imprint of Penguin Random House LLC, 2023

Text copyright © 2023 by Chelsea Clinton
Illustrations copyright © 2023 by Alexandra Boiger

Visit us online at PenguinRandomHouse.com.

Library of Congress Cataloging-in-Publication Data is available.

HC ISBN 9780593620694
PB ISBN 9780593620700

1st Printing

Printed in the United States of America

LSCC

Edited by Talia Benamy and Jill Santopolo.
Design by Ellice M. Lee.
Text set in LTC Kennerley Pro.

To
Deb and her family and
all the fierce girls who will follow

DEAR READER,

As Sally Ride and Marian Wright Edelman both powerfully said, "You can't be what you can't see." When Sally said that, she meant that it was hard to dream of being an astronaut, like she was, or a doctor or an athlete or anything at all if you didn't see someone like you who already had lived that dream. She especially was talking about seeing women in jobs that historically were held by men.

I wrote the first *She Persisted* and the books that came after it because I wanted young girls—and children of all genders—to see women who worked hard to live their dreams. And I wanted all of us to see examples of persistence in the face of different challenges to help inspire us in our own lives.

I'm so thrilled now to partner with a sisterhood of writers to bring longer, more in-depth versions of these stories of women's persistence and achievement to readers. I hope you enjoy these chapter books as much as I do and find them inspiring and empowering.

And remember: If anyone ever tells you no, if anyone ever says your voice isn't important or your dreams are too big, remember these women. They persisted and so should you.

Warmly,

Chelsea Clinton

She
Persisted

....

She Persisted: MARIAN ANDERSON

She Persisted: VIRGINIA APGAR

She Persisted: PURA BELPRÉ

She Persisted: SIMONE BILES

She Persisted: NELLIE BLY

She Persisted: RUBY BRIDGES

She Persisted: KALPANA CHAWLA

She Persisted: CLAUDETTE COLVIN

She Persisted: ELLA FITZGERALD

She Persisted: ROSALIND FRANKLIN

She Persisted: TEMPLE GRANDIN

She Persisted: DEB HAALAND

She Persisted: BETHANY HAMILTON

She Persisted: DOROTHY HEIGHT

She Persisted: FLORENCE GRIFFITH JOYNER

She Persisted: HELEN KELLER

She Persisted: CORETTA SCOTT KING

She Persisted: CLARA LEMLICH

She Persisted: RACHEL LEVINE

She Persisted: MAYA LIN

She Persisted: WANGARI MAATHAI

She Persisted: WILMA MANKILLER

She Persisted: PATSY MINK

She Persisted: FLORENCE NIGHTINGALE

She Persisted: SALLY RIDE

She Persisted: MARGARET CHASE SMITH

She Persisted: SONIA SOTOMAYOR

She Persisted: MARIA TALLCHIEF

She Persisted: DIANA TAURASI

She Persisted: HARRIET TUBMAN

She Persisted: OPRAH WINFREY

She Persisted: MALALA YOUSAFZAI

DEB HAALAND

TABLE OF CONTENTS

....

· ·

Destined to Serve

W hen Debra "Deb" Haaland was a child, she never would have dreamed she would become one of the most powerful Native women in the United States government. Deb says, "I wasn't the type of child that said, 'Oh, I want to be a congresswoman when I grow up. I want to be president.' I never said any of that." But she would rise to the top, and her Native voice would be heard.

Debra Anne Haaland was born in Winslow, Arizona, on December 2, 1960. Deb's mother, Mary Elizabeth Toya, was a citizen of the Pueblo of Laguna, a Native Nation in New Mexico. Deb's dad, John David "Dutch" Haaland, was a Norwegian American born in New London, Minnesota, whose grandparents had immigrated to the United States from Koivisto, Norway.

Deb's parents were both in the military, stationed at Treasure Island military base in San Francisco, California, where they met and married. Deb's mom was in the navy and Deb's dad was in the Marine Corps.

Deb had two older sisters named Denise and Zoe, and a younger brother named John. Since they were a military family, they moved around a lot. The Haaland family moved to a different base almost every two years, traveling across the country from Quantico, Virginia, to Oceanside, California, and to their homeland at the Pueblo of Laguna in New Mexico. They moved so much that Deb went to thirteen different public schools as a child.

At each of the places they moved, Deb's dad would always make sure to take the children outside to enjoy nature. They would take walks on the beach in California and hike the sandy desert trails in New Mexico.

Even though Deb's family moved so much, she never got too upset by it. The family packed up whenever they were ordered to. Deb made new friends and lived in new homes and neighborhoods each time she moved. Deb considered herself a "military brat" because she was able to get used

to all the changes easily with each new situation.

When Deb's mom left the navy, she began working for the Bureau of Indian Affairs (BIA). The BIA is part of the Department of the Interior in the United States government, and its role today is to help the government work with Native Nations and provide services they need. There, she provided educational services to Natives and Alaskan Natives as a teacher's aide, secretary, and later office manager for the superintendent of schools.

Deb's dad stayed on as an officer in the United States Marine Corps for thirty years. During this time, he spent two years fighting in the Vietnam War, where he saved six men's lives while risking his own. Dutch was awarded two Purple Hearts and a Silver Star for his bravery in Vietnam. While her father was away at war, Deb and her sisters and brother would write him letters almost every day. Writing letters helps soldiers and their families keep connected from far away. Even though Deb missed him, she understood that he couldn't be with their family because he had a big responsibility to do his duty

in the military. She learned from both of her parents what service to her country meant.

After Deb's dad came back from Vietnam, the family would gather at the kitchen table to watch the evening news. Deb would sometimes see her dad cry when the news of the Vietnam War came on. When she grew up, she understood how hard it must have been to go to war.

In between different moves that Deb's family made across the country, the Pueblo of Laguna always drew them home. Deb's grandparents lived there, and Deb's mom ensured that they would always have a connection to their Native community. Deb's time there gave her some of the best years of her childhood.

·······························

Home Is Where the Heart Is

The Pueblo of Laguna is about seventy miles west of Albuquerque, New Mexico. Albuquerque is the largest city in New Mexico, while Laguna Pueblo is a smaller Native community, a town in the open desert near mountains. Pueblo means "village" in Spanish. Laguna Pueblo is one of nineteen pueblos in New Mexico, each with its own separate Native government, modern homes, and people working both in the community and in nearby cities.

Like all Native tribal nations, the Pueblo of Laguna is a sovereign nation. "Sovereign" means that tribes run their own governments and make their own decisions about their communities. Each Native Nation is considered a nation within a nation—that is, a Native Nation within the larger United States nation. Native people who belong to sovereign tribal Nations are citizens of both. In Deb's case, she is a citizen of the Pueblo of Laguna and a citizen of the United States.

The United States is very new compared to Native tribes and Nations. Deb's ancestors lived in the Pueblo of Laguna for thousands of years before the United States became a country. Deb likes to say she is a thirty-fifth generation New Mexican!

Deb's mother made sure her children were connected to their Laguna Pueblo homeland and grandparents growing up. Deb's grandparents on her mother's side lived in both the Pueblo of Laguna and Winslow, Arizona. Native people often move to cities to work, and when they have ancestral homelands, they often go back to see family and community and for special occasions. Homelands have a special place in people's hearts and have a sacred pull that never lets go.

Deb's grandparents were farmers from the small village of Mesita in Laguna Pueblo, where there is an agricultural tradition of harvesting vegetables from the land and living near the rivers that offer water. Mesita means "small table" in Spanish. The Laguna name for the village is Tsé Ch´ééhii, which means "red rocks pointing out horizontally."

There was no electricity in Deb's grandparents' one-room family home, so they relied on a clay-brick oven for heat and cooking. Deb's grandmother did not like kids in the kitchen getting in the way while she cooked, so when Deb was very young, she steered clear. Still interested in what her grandmother was doing, though, she would watch through a kitchen window. Later

she would copy what she saw her grandmother do: baking bread, cooking beans and chiles, and preparing fresh vegetables, including the ones her grandfather grew. Today Deb says she is proud that her grandparents' growing and cooking methods have been passed down to her, and now she passes them down to her child.

Back then, Deb's grandma would ask her to haul water from the village well because there was no running water in the family home. Deb would go to the middle of the village, fill two buckets to the brim, and carry them the length of four football fields back home. The family used the water for drinking and bathing. They would fill a tub with water, and Deb would take a turn bathing after her six cousins had already used the same water. Deb learned that every drop of water she carried was precious and should not be wasted.

Deb and her grandpa spent their summers in the garden. She would help him pick worms off corn and pull weeds in his cornfields. While Deb's grandpa watered the peach orchard, Deb would sit in the shade of a peach tree and listen to the whistle of passing trains. A breeze would cool her off while she ate sweet fruit.

Deb's grandfather also taught her the tradition of respecting the life of all animals. When her grandfather brought home a deer that he had hunted, he took the deer's body to the garage and slept overnight with it until the deer's spirit left.

As Deb grew older, her grandmother and mother shared terrible stories about Indian boarding schools. In 1881, Deb's great-grandfather was taken to Carlisle Indian Industrial School in

Pennsylvania, almost two thousand miles away from New Mexico. The school motto was "Kill the Indian . . . and save the man." It was one of many government- and church-run schools that existed back then with the goal of trying to make the children who were forced to attend them feel ashamed of being Native. Those schools weren't interested in giving children a real education. They were trying to erase Native cultures by reeducating their children in harmful ways by erasing their Native languages, stories, and cultures. The adults running the schools sometimes physically hurt the children too. Tragically, many children who attended those schools were treated so poorly that they died.

These Indian boarding schools stayed up and running for many years, long past when Deb's great-grandfather was a child. The government also took Deb's grandparents to one of these types of schools in Santa Fe, New Mexico, from when they were eight to when they were thirteen. This was where they first met. Her grandpa was from a nearby pueblo named Jemez. Her grandmother was one of many children from Laguna Pueblo who were gathered up by a Catholic priest and put on a train. She was lonely and missed her family.

Deb's grandma mostly spent her days cleaning and cooking, not learning. She ironed clothes and peeled potatoes. Her father visited her just two times during these five years, as the school was so far away by horse and wagon.

By the 1960s, most of the Indian boarding schools across the nation had stopped operating, and the Native cultures had survived. But Deb heard the stories, and she learned how unfairly Native people had been treated. These injustices taught Deb that her family and community had a resiliency, or a toughness, rooted in their Native culture that gave them the strength not to give up who they were. Deb would later say that she was a product of these Indian boarding schools, and they would inspire her to be fierce later in life when she began to serve her country.

CHAPTER 3

· ·

Laguna Feast Days

Deb's childhood in Laguna with her grand-parents greatly influenced her. She grew up in and around her family's traditional home-lands, learning the importance of water, protect-ing resources, and having a deep respect for the earth. She heard family stories that made them all stronger. Deb lived her mother's mantra: "Don't waste, and be careful with the things that keep us alive." Deb also learned a lot about her culture through feast days in Laguna Pueblo.

The Pueblo of Laguna has several feast day celebrations and ceremonies. These days are filled with songs and dances in the village's central plaza. As a child, Deb loved to participate by dancing at feast day ceremonies—she even danced when she was the only one in her family to do so! She was very dedicated to the cultural traditions of her pueblo.

Feast days often mix the religious traditions of the Native communities with Catholic traditions that were introduced by the Spanish a few hundred years ago. The Native people dance for the land, for rain, for corn, for animals, and for all people. At the same time, they honor the pueblo's Catholic patron saints. In Mesita, for instance, the community celebrates the Assumption of Our Blessed Mother's Feast Day each year on August 15.

On feast days, all the dancers, drummers, and singers, including Deb when she danced, wear traditional clothing. The girls wear black dresses fastened over the shoulder on one side. These dresses are called mantas. Underneath a manta there is a colorful cotton dress with bright, streaming ribbons. Red, green, and black woven sashes cinch it at the waist. Girls also wear white deerskin moccasins that start at their feet and wrap up to their knees like leggings, and shiny turquoise-and-coral necklaces dangle around their necks.

In the plaza, surrounded by warm red adobe homes, a long line of brightly dressed dancers gather, from the very young to the elderly. They all dance to the rhythm of the drums and singers.

They hold small cedar branches, feathers, and gourd rattles that sway up and down. The dancers, community, and guests all receive the blessings of the ceremonial dances throughout the day.

During breaks, the community invites guests into their adobe homes for traditional meals, such as chile stews, beans, vegetable dishes from the garden, and tamales. Deb's grandmother would cook for hundreds of people during feast days. Deb's family taught her the importance of preparing food and sharing it. It was not just that they wanted to feed hungry people, but that they understood that the nourishment of a person's soul and heart is a way to share a culture.

When they weren't home in Laguna, Deb's mom always made sure she passed on their pueblo values and traditional wisdom. As an adult, Deb said, "You can be Native wherever you are." This means that all Native people carry their cultures anywhere they may live. It was a message that Deb definitely took to heart throughout her life, wherever she went.

CHAPTER 4

Working Hard

When Deb was a teenager, she and her family moved to Albuquerque, New Mexico. There she attended Highland High School. When she was fourteen, she got her first job at a family-owned business called Zinn's Bakery. She decorated cakes and worked the cash register, taking payments from customers.

Deb continued working at the bakery after graduating high school. She had learned a lot from

Mr. and Mrs. Zinn, including how to be a hard worker. Even so, one morning she asked herself, *Am I going to be doing this for the rest of my life?*

It was then that Deb had the idea to go to college. Growing up, no one had ever encouraged her to even think about it. Her parents hadn't gone to college, and it wasn't something she had ever thought she might do. But once she got her mind set on it, there was no stopping her. Deb's mother had a friend at the Bureau of Indian Affairs who helped Deb figure out how to apply. At age twenty-eight, Deb was accepted to the University of New Mexico in Albuquerque.

Deb liked writing, so she became an English major. She would do extra assignments, like attending lectures beyond the ones she had to go to for her classes, to help her grades. She went

to a special talk by John Echohawk, a man who worked for the American Indian Rights Fund, an organization that protects Natives' rights. Deb also took a political science class taught by Fred Harris. Mr. Harris had served as a United States senator, making laws to help our county run smoothly. These two experiences helped Deb see that she might want to study law after finishing her English degree.

It was not always easy being the first in her family to attend college. At times she struggled to pay for it, so she borrowed money to stay in school. Graduating was a big accomplishment! Deb was ready to graduate in 1994, when she was thirty-four. Four days after graduation, she gave birth to her beautiful baby girl, Somáh. Deb was a single mom by choice. She firmly believed that all women should have choices about how they live their lives.

After graduation, Deb started a company

called Pueblo Salsa. Her business required her to take trips all around New Mexico. Deb and little Somáh would hit the road blasting their music. Their travels took them to the Hatch Valley in southern New Mexico. There, Deb would buy the famous Hatch green chiles that have a spicy and smoky flavor. They were the main ingredient in Pueblo Salsa. Deb sold jarred salsa to small mom-and-pop grocery stores, state fairs, and fiery food shows.

As Somáh got a bit older, Deb wanted her to go to preschool. Preschool would offer early education for Deb's daughter, but it was also expensive for a single mom. She found a preschool that let her pay a reduced fee in exchange for cleaning the building. As Deb worked hard cleaning the preschool at night, she realized that there were

probably other struggling mothers who were not finding the type of support they needed.

Around the same time that she realized this, something else happened that made Deb begin to see the power of the Native vote in US elections and how those elections might help struggling mothers like her. She had heard about the Lakota Nation coming out in record numbers to vote and changing the outcome of a political race in South Dakota. Because of the Lakota Nation, South Dakota now had a Democratic senator, which was a big change. And it meant better support for the Lakota Nation and others who were struggling. Deb was amazed at what a difference voting could make and thought, *I bet we could do this here.*

It was time to set a new goal. Fred Harris had inspired Deb with his political science class, and she turned to him now with her idea: she wanted to study the law. With his help, Deb got into law school. She sold her Pueblo Salsa business and started down this next path on her journey.

CHAPTER 5

· ·

Warming Up Her Voice

Deb's law professors said that she was an excellent student. Although Deb's classes were going well, she struggled at times to afford things for herself and her daughter. Deb applied for food stamps, which is a government program to help families that don't have enough money for food. One time, Deb didn't have enough money to rent an apartment. She and Somáh stayed with friends until she could afford to rent one again.

But even with her struggles, Deb remained pos-itive, made her daughter feel safe, and worked hard, and they both persisted as Deb graduated law school in 2006.

After graduation, Deb took an important state test called the New Mexico Bar Exam. If she passed, it would let her practice law in New Mexico. She failed by a few points, but that did not keep Deb from finding her path to public service. A law school professor encouraged her to apply for a training program called Emerge New Mexico. Deb was accepted, and the program gave her the tools to run for public office.

Deb took action to make sure that Native people understood the importance of voting. In 2004, she volunteered for Democratic presiden-tial candidate John Kerry by calling Natives on the phone to encourage them to vote. After that, in 2008, she volunteered for Barack Obama when he ran for president. He won! For President Obama's second presidential election, Deb was hired as the New Mexico Native vote director. Deb traveled all over the state of New Mexico asking people to vote for President Obama. She focused on tribal communities by knocking on doors and encouraging adults to register and vote. People in the communities she visited responded to Deb because she looked like them, had similar struggles, and listened. Deb began to bring communities into the Democratic Party that hadn't felt accepted before.

It wasn't always easy to get people to vote. Some Native people don't trust the government because of how unfairly Native people have been and are often still treated. Deb would gather Native people in community halls and bring big pots of green and red chile stew and a stack of tortillas. As her grandmother had shown her years earlier, food helped bring people together.

Deb found that storytelling was helpful too. She told the story of a Native man, Sergeant Miguel Trujillo from Isleta Pueblo, who served as a marine in World War II. He returned home to New Mexico a hero, yet he wasn't allowed to vote. Native people born in the United States had been granted citizenship in 1924, but that hadn't fixed everything. In 1947, the New Mexico Constitution did not give Natives who lived on reservations, the land set aside for Native Nations, the right to vote. Trujillo sued the state government, and the law was changed the next year. The history of Natives is not often well-known, even to other Native people. Deb's storytelling helped people understand how hard Trujillo fought for their right to vote today. And knowing that made the Native Americans she was talking to realize that they should vote too.

After President Obama's second election, Deb went to work for big tribal businesses. She also became the first woman elected to the Laguna Pueblo board of directors. As the board chair-woman, she oversaw the tribal casino and adopted new environmental and energy policies. Next, she became a tribal administrator at San Felipe Pueblo, which is another one of New Mexico's nineteen pueblos.

Then Deb decided to help in another way and enter a political race of her own. In 2014, she

ran for lieutenant governor of New Mexico. She lost, but that did not stop Deb from persisting! She turned her attention to running for chair of the Democratic Party of New Mexico—and this time she won! She served as chair from 2015 to 2017 and was the first Native person to ever hold this position.

In 2016, Deb started to hear about something big happening in North Dakota. Members of the Standing Rock Sioux Tribe, along with other Native demonstrators and their supporters, had gathered to protest the construction of the Dakota Access Pipeline, an oil pipeline that was threatening the Standing Rock Sioux Tribe's main water supply and sacred lands. This movement became known as NoDAPL or No Dakota Access Pipeline.

Deb traveled to the protestors' camp and joined them. Again, she cooked green chile stew and offered a Pueblo meal while listening and talking to the community. She called on all Indigenous peoples to support the protest. Unfortunately, the pipeline was built. The protesters may have lost their fight, but they did not lose their determination. This protest was one of the largest gatherings of Native tribes in more than a century. Native people felt empowered and felt they had a voice. Deb said, "It caused a lot of folks to say, 'You know what? People need to listen to Native Americans.'"

The next year, 104 Natives ran for public office in the United States. This was a record-breaking number of Natives who wanted to represent their communities. One of those people was Deb. She ran to represent New Mexico in the House of Representatives. The House of Representatives is one of the two parts of the US Congress, where laws are made that impact people everywhere. No Native woman had ever been a US representative, and Deb was ready to be the first.

It was time to gear up for another election.

CHAPTER 6

··································

I'll Be Fierce for All of Us

D eb ran a long and hard campaign, and in
the end, she won! She and Sharice Davids,
who is a citizen of the Ho-Chunk Nation of
Wisconsin and was elected the same year to represent Kansas, were sworn into the US House of
Representatives in January 2019. They became
the first Native women ever to be in Congress.
On the day she was sworn in, Deb said, "As a
kid, I never could have imagined today. I will

leave a ladder down behind me so girls of color know they can be anything they want to be."

Deb brought a bipartisan perspective to Congress. To be bipartisan is to have cooperation and compromise between the two major political parties, Democrats and Republicans. Most Native Nation leadership traditionally believe in listening to all community ideas before making a decision. By listening, you can discover what you and other people have in common. This makes it easier to solve problems and reach a positive outcome for all. Plus, Deb had an auntie named Ann who taught her to always be nice to everyone. All of that made her really want to take everyone's ideas and opinions to heart.

Deb's bipartisan attitude was so successful that she passed the most bills out of all freshmen her first year in Congress. Writing and passing a bill is the most important job of any congress-person. Bills can become laws if a majority of people in both the House of Representatives and the Senate vote for them, and if they are then approved by the president. The president signed five of Deb's bills. And four of the bills helped Native communities with their government, their businesses, their safety, and their healthcare.

Despite her success in Congress, though, she didn't stay there for long. A new path was waiting for Deb—another first. In 2020, newly elected president Joe Biden selected a unique group of people to be in his cabinet. The cabinet is like a group of team captains working together to help the president run the country. Most of the people in a president's cabinet are called secretaries.

Deb would become the first Native person to hold a cabinet position and the first Native to be nominated as the Secretary of the Interior. When it was first created, the Department of the Interior had cruel policies that hurt Native people and took their land. Today, the Department of the Interior protects public lands, increases environmental protections, and works to strengthen its nation-to-nation relationship with Native tribes. Now Deb would lead that department! She would be a new leader with new ideas. Deb promised to work with Native Nations and invite them to meetings so their voices would be heard.

Deb was sworn in as Secretary of the Interior in March 2021 wearing Native clothing: a rainbow-striped ribbon skirt adorned with butterflies, stars, and corn; moccasins with tall white deerskin leggings; a concho silver belt and turquoise necklace; and dragonfly earrings. Every time she wears Native fashion, Deb is stating with pride, "We [Native people] are still here." Deb's sisters and her longtime partner and fiancé, Skip Sayre, were standing beside her, and her daughter, Somáh, held the Bible on which her mom took the oath of office. Deb was sworn in by Vice President Kamala Harris. She stated, "Growing up in my mother's Pueblo household made me fierce. I'll be fierce for all of us, our planet, and all of our protected land. I am honored and ready to serve."

Three weeks after being sworn into office, Deb went to the state of Utah to visit Bears Ear and Grand Staircase–Escalante National Monuments. These monuments are sacred to Natives and were under threat of being destroyed by oil, gas, and uranium mining development. Deb listened to the state and tribal leaders and environmentalists' different views and reported back to President Biden. President Biden valued the Native perspective, and he decided to protect these national monuments for all Americans.

Next, Deb announced an investigation into what had happened to Native children like her grandparents and great-grandfather who had been taken away to boarding schools. Deb knew that the process would be difficult. It is sad to know that our country took children away from their families, and Deb recognized that these families deserved to know what happened to their loved ones. To become a better nation, it is important to admit these painful truths and understand the

hurt caused to Native families over generations and centuries. That investigation is still ongoing as of 2023.

As Secretary of the Interior, Deb is serving her country just as her parents did. Deb thanks the generations of ancestors who came before her and who sacrificed so much so that she can be here today to act on behalf of all of us. When she protects lands and the environment, she may remember helping her grandfather in his cornfields and hauling the precious water to her grandmother's home. She may see the orange-and-red mesa stretch to the blue sky in the Pueblo of Laguna, where her grandparents taught her the importance of living with the land and water. From her grandmother's pueblo home in New Mexico to the halls of power in Washington, DC,

Deb always believed in working hard and helping others. Today, she continues to work fiercely for a better future for everyone—and to show us all that a better future is possible, as long as we persist.

HOW YOU CAN PERSIST

by Laurel Goodluck

Deb found her voice and now uses it to represent all people and the land. Here are some ideas of how you can use your voice too.

1. Ask your grandparents, aunts, uncles, or elders to tell stories of your family or community. From the stories, you may learn how they made decisions to be stronger.

2. When you have a conversation, listen without interrupting and then repeat what the other person said. Then you take a turn, and the other person listens and repeats. Listening helps you be a good leader by respecting others and helping them to feel heard.

3. Learn our country's entire history. Unfortunately, Native history after the 1890s is often not included in school lessons. You can start by learning what tribal Nations are in your state and researching their specific histories. Understanding America's history will help us deal with new issues we face as a nation. And remember, Natives are still here.

4. Think of the cultural activities in your family, such as family events and celebrations. You may speak your culture's language. These cultural traditions can give you strength and pride and help you know who you are. Celebrate different cultures in your community by attending their public events.

5. You know your community the best and what its needs are because you live there. Think about what you care most about in your community and volunteer to do some good. Some children have planted trees to help the environment, collected coats for others in need, volunteered at a food bank,

raised money for an animal shelter, made signs for election candidates, and so much more. You decide!

6. Voting is one of the best ways to make your voice heard and stand up for what you believe in! You can ask your parent or teacher to get a sample ballot before Election Day and have them review the candidates' ideas. Ask your parent or another grown-up in your life to bring you with them to vote, and ask if you can pull the lever, push the button, or help feed your ballot into the machine. After all the votes are in, find out how the election turned out.

7. Don't let fear of not understanding another person or idea stop you from

being open to the beauty of diverse experiences and perspectives. The more people with different ideas who come together to solve a problem, the more possible solutions you can find. You can explore new ideas and people by reading more books with diverse main characters and settings. You will be able to experience the similarities you share, learn another person's way of doing things, and, best of all, have an adventure with a good story.

8. Cherish the outdoors by going outside and enjoying nature. Play, take walks, ride your bike, and daydream. You can also become a good steward of your environment. This means taking care

of the land and animals with love.
You can do this in many ways, such
as picking up trash, feeding the birds,
growing vegetables, trees, and flowers,
and taking care of your pets.

9. Have courage by not being afraid to be
   first, try something new, or speak up
   for what you believe in. Your voice and
   actions matter.

NOTES ON TERMS

by Traci Sorell, adapted by Laurel Goodluck

"Indian," "American Indian," "Pueblo Indian," "Native American," "Native," and "Indigenous" are all used to describe the peoples who originally lived on this land and continue to do so, even since the formation of the United States.

The label "Indian" came from Christopher Columbus. He wrongly believed he had landed on the Indian sub-continent, instead of encountering Taíno people on the Caribbean island that the countries of the Dominican Republic and Haiti now share. As a result of his error, "Indian" became the word commonly used. When the Spanish arrived in the early 1500s in the Southwest, they called the Native people Pueblo Indians. "Pueblo" in Span-ish can refer to "townspeople," which the Spanish believed described the villages.

Sometimes "American" is added before "Indian" or the term "Native American" is used, but these are incor-rect too. Native Nations and their citizens lived on this big continent long before it was given the name "America." This happened because Italian navigator Amerigo Vespucci sailed around the large landmass and realized it was a separate continent and not part of Asia.

More recently, "Native people," "Natives," "Indigenous," and "Indigenous peoples" are words used to describe the original people of this land. But it's important to remember that all those people come from a variety of Nations and have specific names that they call themselves, which is the best way to refer to them. For example, Deb Haaland's Nation is the Pueblo of Laguna. In their own Keres language, they refer to themselves as "K'awaika."

ACKNOWLEDGMENTS

....

Deb Haaland had a strong culture, community, mother, grand-mother, and later a more extensive network of people who helped her find her path and voice. I also have many people in my network who helped me tell the story of how Deb became fierce for all of us.

Thank you, Traci Sorell, for recommending me to write this book. Your mentorship through WNDB was life-changing. Your guidance and belief in me have steered me to a nest of Native kidlit community that is becoming a force of storytellers.

I am grateful to my agent, Nicole Geiger, whose support is never-ending. Thank you for your expert editing skills, gentle soundboard, and belief in my voice and stories. I love being part of the Full Circle Literary family.

I admire Chelsea Clinton's vision of She Persisted for young readers. I am grateful to the Persisterhood that is bring-ing a unique voice forward. It has been an honor to be part of the fantastic team at Philomel, beginning with the warm welcome and later expert edits from Jill Santopolo and Talia Benamy.

Thank you to the Indigenous women who have paved the way for Deb in Washington, DC, including fierce women in my family. These include my late aunty Phyllis Old Dog Cross, who served as an air force flight nurse during the Korean War and was appointed to Jimmy Carter's Presidential Commission on Mental Health as a psychiatric nurse serving Native communities in 1977. They also include my sister, Karen Atkinson, an attorney, who had a long career advocating for Native people in Washington, DC, in senior leadership positions for the Department of the Interior, the Department of Energy, and Native nonprofits. It all began when she joined the Clinton administration in the late 1990s and was the first Native American appointed to a non–Indian Affairs office, bringing Native voices that were lacking before to agency decisions in the governmental system. Next, my fierce aunty Carol Juneau, who served as a member of both branches of the Montana legislature from 1999 to 2011. She was instrumental in the groundbreaking passage of Indian Education for All in 1999 and was a tireless advocate for Native voting rights. And my cousin Denise Juneau, who was the first Native woman to hold a state constitutional office as superintendent of public instruction for Montana from 2009 to 2017. In 2016 she bravely ran for Congress but lost. Last, my cousin Patricia Mattingly, who had a long federal career, held leadership roles, and is currently serving through a BIA appointment as director of the bureau's Southwest Regional Office.

To my husband, Dr. Kevin Goodluck, for always saying, "We have a good life." To my grown boys, Kalen and Forrest, who have inspired my storytelling journey with their life ambitions as a journalist and photographer and an actor and filmmaker, respectively.

I've had constant and unconditional love and support from my mother and late father. As a child, they set up a community of aunties, uncles, and cousins and an intertribal circle of friends that surrounded my sister and me and made us confident and fearless. They passed on a love for our homeland and culture, a belief in education, a curiosity to travel and explore, and the freedom to try new and different things. For my parents, I will be forever grateful.

⁀ References ⊷

Clinton, Chelsea. "Environmental Justice (with Sec. Deb Haaland, Dr. Mona Hanna-Attisha & Juan Parras)." *In Fact with Chelsea Clinton.* Podcast. May 4, 2021. omny.fm/shows/in-fact-with-chelsea-clinton-1/environmental-justice-with-sec-deb-haaland-dr-mona?in_playlist =podcast.

Fadel, Leila, and Talia Wiener. "Record Number of Native Americans Running for Office in Midterms." NPR. July 4, 2018. npr.org/2018/07/04/625425037/record-number-of-native-americans-running-for-office-in-midterms.

Haaland, Deb. "Deb Haaland: My Grandparents Were Stolen from Their Families as Children. We Must Learn about This History." *The Washington Post*. June 11, 2021. washingtonpost.com/opinions/2021/06/11/deb-haaland-indigenous-boarding-schools.

McGrady, Clyde. "Former 'Military Brat' Deb Haaland Honors Dad at Marine Corps Marathon." *Roll Call*. October 30, 2019. rollcall.com/2019/10/30/former-military-brat-deb-haaland-honors-dad-at-marine-corps-marathon.

McGrady, Clyde. "Haaland Recalls Struggles as Single Mom, Thanksgiving and Being Homeless." *Roll Call*. September 16, 2019. rollcall.com/2019/09/16/haaland-recalls-struggles-as-single-mom-thanksgiving-and-being-homeless.

Monet, Jenni. "Deb Haaland, a Living Testament."
Sierra. September 15, 2021. sierraclub.org
/sierra/2021-4-fall/feature/deb-haaland-living
-testament.

Narducci, Vincent. "Deb Haaland: One for the
History Books." *Mirage Magazine*. November
3, 2021. mirage.unm.edu/deb-haaland-one-for
-the-history-books.

NBC News. "Rep. Deb Haaland: 'We Can't
Take Our Democracy for Granted' | NBC
News." YouTube. August 21, 2020. Video,
2:38. youtube.com/watch?v=55HPj5uVYXs.

Nelson, Rebecca. "Native American Women
Made History in the Midterms. Here's Why
It Took So Long." *Newsweek*. November 9, 2018.
newsweek.com/native-american-women-congress
-history-midterms-1207991.

NoiseCat, Julian Brave. "What a Joe Biden
Cabinet Pick Might Mean for Native
Americans—and Democrats." Politico.
November 30, 2020. politico.com/news
/magazine/2020/11/30/deb-haaland-native
-americans-interior-biden-440916.

TEDx Talks. "Who Speaks for You? | Debra
Haaland | TEDxABQ." YouTube. December
22, 2016. Video, 7:49. youtube.com/watch?v
=KkEY6zaqdlM.

Trahant, Mark. "Meet the Native Americans
Running for Office in 2018." *High Country
News.* August 3, 2018. hcn.org/articles
/election-2018-here-are-the-native-americans
-running-for-office-2018.

LAUREL GOODLUCK writes picture books that reflect Native children's cultural experiences and everyday life, showing Native children that they have a perspective that is unique and powerful. She is the author of *Forever Cousins* and *Rock Your Mocs*. Raised in the San Francisco Bay Area, Laurel comes from an intertribal background of Mandan and Hidatsa from the prairies of North Dakota and Tsimshian from a rainforest in Alaska. She now lives in Albuquerque, New Mexico, with her Navajo husband, where they raised two children also bent on storytelling in journalism and acting.

Photo credit: Forrest Goodluck

You can visit Laurel Goodluck online at
LaurelGoodluck.com
or follow her on Twitter and Instagram
@LaurieGoodluck

GILLIAN FLINT has worked as a professional illustrator since earning an animation and illustration degree in 2003. Her work has since been published in the UK, USA and Australia. In her spare time, Gillian enjoys reading, spending time with her family and puttering about in the garden on sunny days. She lives in the northwest of England.

You can visit Gillian Flint online at
gillianflint.com
or follow her on Instagram
@gillianflint_illustration

CHELSEA CLINTON is the author of the #1 *New York Times* bestseller *She Persisted: 13 American Women Who Changed the World*; *She Persisted Around the World: 13 Women Who Changed History*; *She Persisted in Sports: American Olympians Who Changed the Game*; *Don't Let Them Disappear: 12 Endangered Species Across the Globe*; *It's Your World: Get Informed, Get Inspired & Get Going!*; *Start Now!: You Can Make a Difference*; with Hillary Clinton, *Grandma's Gardens* and *Gutsy Women*; and, with Devi Sridhar, *Governing Global Health: Who Runs the World and Why?* She is also the Vice Chair of the Clinton Foundation, where she works on many initiatives, including those that help empower the next generation of leaders. She lives in New York City with her husband, Marc, their children and their dog, Soren.

You can follow Chelsea Clinton on Twitter
@ChelseaClinton
or on Facebook at
facebook.com/chelseaclinton

ALEXANDRA BOIGER has illustrated nearly twenty picture books, including the She Persisted books by Chelsea Clinton; the popular Tallulah series by Marilyn Singer; and the Max and Marla books, which she also wrote. Originally from Munich, Germany, she now lives outside of San Francisco, California, with her husband, Andrea, daughter, Vanessa, and two cats, Luiso and Winter.

You can visit Alexandra Boiger online at
alexandraboiger.com
or follow her on Instagram
@alexandra_boiger

Read about more inspiring women in the

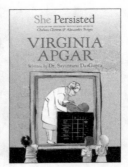

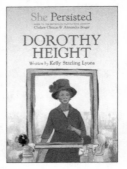

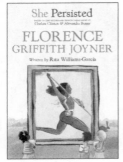

She Persisted series!

She Persisted

BASED ON THE BESTSELLING PICTURE BOOK INSPIRED BY
Chelsea Clinton & Alexandra Boiger

RACHEL
LEVINE

Written by Lisa Bunker

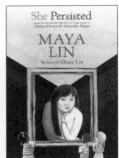

She Persisted

BASED ON THE BESTSELLING PICTURE BOOK INSPIRED BY
Chelsea Clinton & Alexandra Boiger

MAYA
LIN

Written by Grace Lin

She Persisted

BASED ON THE BESTSELLING PICTURE BOOK INSPIRED BY
Chelsea Clinton & Alexandra Boiger

WANGARI
MAATHAI

Written by Eucabeth Odhiambo

She Persisted

BASED ON THE BESTSELLING PICTURE BOOK INSPIRED BY
Chelsea Clinton & Alexandra Boiger

SALLY
RIDE

Written by Atia Abawi

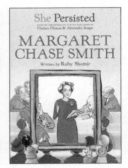

She Persisted

BASED ON THE BESTSELLING PICTURE BOOK INSPIRED BY
Chelsea Clinton & Alexandra Boiger

MARGARET
CHASE SMITH

Written by Ruby Shamir

She Persisted

BASED ON THE BESTSELLING PICTURE BOOK INSPIRED BY
Chelsea Clinton & Alexandra Boiger

SONIA
SOTOMAYOR

Written by Meg Medina

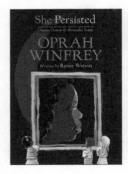

She Persisted

BASED ON THE BESTSELLING PICTURE BOOK INSPIRED BY
Chelsea Clinton & Alexandra Boiger

OPRAH
WINFREY

Written by Renée Watson

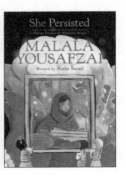

She Persisted

BASED ON THE BESTSELLING PICTURE BOOK INSPIRED BY
Chelsea Clinton & Alexandra Boiger

MALALA
YOUSAFZAI

Written by Aisha Saeed

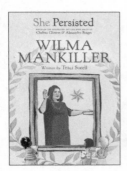

She Persisted
BASED ON THE BESTSELLING PICTURE BOOK BY
Chelsea Clinton & Alexandra Boiger

WILMA
MANKILLER
Written by Traci Sorell

She Persisted
BASED ON THE BESTSELLING PICTURE BOOK BY
Chelsea Clinton & Alexandra Boiger

PATSY
MINK
Written by Tae Keller

She Persisted
BASED ON THE BESTSELLING PICTURE BOOK BY
Chelsea Clinton & Alexandra Boiger

FLORENCE
NIGHTINGALE
Written by Shelli R. Johannes

She Persisted
BASED ON THE BESTSELLING PICTURE BOOK BY
Chelsea Clinton & Alexandra Boiger

MARIA
TALLCHIEF
Written by Christine Day

She Persisted
BASED ON THE BESTSELLING PICTURE BOOK BY
Chelsea Clinton & Alexandra Boiger

DIANA
TAURASI
Written by Monica Brown

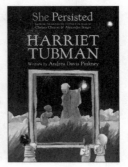

She Persisted
BASED ON THE BESTSELLING PICTURE BOOK BY
Chelsea Clinton & Alexandra Boiger

HARRIET
TUBMAN
Written by Andrea Davis Pinkney